ELIOT SHUN

CRUSH IT WITH KINDLE

The Essential Guide to Kindle Marketing, Discover Strategies and Tricks On How to Effectively Write and Market Your eBooks

Descrierea CIP a Bibliotecii Naționale a României
ELIOT SHUN
    CRUSH IT WITH KINDLE. The Essential Guide to Kindle Marketing, Discover Strategies and Tricks On How to Effectively Write and Market Your eBooks. / Eliot Shun – Bucharest: Editura My Ebook, 2020
    ISBN

ELIOT SHUN

CRUSH IT WITH KINDLE

The Essential Guide to Kindle Marketing, Discover Strategies and Tricks On How to Effectively Write and Market Your eBooks.

My Ebook Publishing House
Bucharest, 2020

TABLE OF CONTENTS

The Kindle Boon

Never before has there been a better time for writers. Never before has there been a better time for people who'd like to build some passive income streams. The Kindle platform allows anyone to publish and earn from their writing. If you do it right, your earnings can match or exceed your current full time income.

It's not that you have to be the next Stephen King or Nora Roberts. Normal writers like you and I are making great strides through Kindle, every day. It used to be relatively easy to just load a bunch a books up to Kindle and make some decent sales. These days, the Amazon algorithm and abundance of Kindle books has changed the game some. You need to do some quality marketing to be seen. No worries - the hardest work will come in the beginning. Then, your work, brand, and books will take off as they would for a new release from any successful writer.

Have you ever published a book for Kindle? Many people have, and have been shocked when it doesn't sell at all. What you read here is going to help you with that.

This book will also help you if you've never published on Kindle at all. Maybe you've just been collecting ebooks on how to be a successful Kindle author but you just haven't taken the plunge yet. This book is going to help you with that, too. It's my goal to help motivate you and inspire you enough to take some massive action. I don't want this to be another Kindle guide that sits there, unused. I want it to be something that transforms you into a successful Kindle author.

You as a Kindle Author

First, I think it's helpful to put yourself into the mindset of a Kindle author. It will be harder for you to get into the groove of things if you don't actually see yourself succeeding with this path. You can't just dream about it - it has to become a reality.

I suggest you start by visiting the Writer's Cafe at Kindle Boards: http://www.kboards.com/index.php/board,60.0.html

Get to know the ups and downs other writers are going through. Be warned, though, that some of the writers know next to nothing about the actual marketing. Some of them are very wary of any marketing at all. But, that's how the Kindle game is played. If you want people to read your high quality fiction or nonfiction books, they need to know about them. There is no shame in getting the word out there about your hard work.

Next, think about the goals you have for yourself as a Kindle author. Do you want to earn just a few hundred extra a month? Are you looking to replace your full time income?

Go ahead and write your goal down. Be very specific - include a dollar amount as well as a time frame. The more specific you are, the better.

You can't succeed with a goal like, "become a successful Kindle author." You can succeed with a goal like, "Earn $1,000 on Kindle within 4 months." Write the goal down and post it somewhere you can see it often.

Are You a Writer?

I'm sure that many people reading this are writers. Maybe you're a ghostwriter looking to branch out and do your own thing. Or, maybe you enjoy writing fiction in your spare time and you'd like to self-publish without dealing with manuscript rejections.

I'm also sure that some people reading this don't consider themselves to be a writer at all. Maybe you've heard a lot of Kindle success stories and you'd like a piece of the pie. That's totally fine. In fact, you can outsource all of the writing and just concentrate on the marketing yourself, if you want to. The only important thing is that the reader receives an outstanding book when they make that purchase.

The Kindle opportunity is there for anyone who wants to take advantage of it. I do want to caution you, however, that you can't just use old PLR or slap some words on a page and expect it to sell. Kindle readers are particularly savvy. They are also tired of spending their money on indie books only to find that they are horribly written or poorly formatted. You don't have to be a fantastic writer, but you do have to provide quality and value, however you go about it.

Kindle has automated systems in place to detect things like PLR and plagiarism, so make sure you steer clear of that, not that you would try it.

Writing Vs. Marketing

Kindle publishing is very unique because you are both the writer and the marketer. As I mentioned earlier, some writers get really discouraged because they just want to write and don't want to do the other stuff. I want to encourage you to move past that mindset. Unless you are extremely lucky, your book isn't going to sell itself.

Yes, Amazon does have systems in place to help authors make sales, but you typically have to get the first several sales yourself...then, you'll go on some of the links on the site. That's part of why I have you consider this a snowball method - the work you do on the front end is really going to help you in the long run.

My goal here is to break the marketing down in a way that is not intimidating, even if you've never done anything like this before.

A self-published Kindle author is both a writer and marketer, so get used to the role.

You're the Publisher

By the same token, you're the publisher. You don't have anyone else to rely on, but yourself. No worries, though, because that's a good thing. You don't have to deal with anyone else but you and Amazon taking a cut of your work. You don't have to deal with rejection...at all. You don't have to deal with the big promises a publisher might make, without delivering.

You get control of it all. Your success will be your own doing and you'll likely be a lot more profitable with it than you would be otherwise. It's exhilarating and exciting to have full control, particularly if you've ever tried the traditional publishing game in the past and gotten frustrated with it. More and more professional authors are moving to doing things on their own, and for good reason.

Traditional Publishers Don't Have it Right

I look at some of the things traditional publishers put out and I'm shocked. They are missing some of the most basic elements of good book marketing. They are stuck in the dark ages of publishing and haven't made any moves to catch up. For instance, many traditionally published books lack cross-promotion, list building, websites, and more. You are going to be far ahead of some traditionally backed authors because you'll have these things in place.

Do This Before Release

This is not a guide on how to write your book - this is a guide on the marketing of it. Still, I will give you a few suggestions. Make sure the book is on a popular topic or popular fiction genre. Take a look at the structure and organization other authors have used in their books on similar topics. Browse through the reviews of these books and note what people liked and did not like about them.

Write your book (or revise it) with these things in mind. You want your work to stand apart as something really great. Don't overcomplicate things - just do good work.

Format the Book

Many people are intimidated by the thought of trying to format their book for Kindle. There are various tools that will do it for you. The easiest is probably the Kinstant Formatter, which is a tool you pay for.

Amazon also has a guide on how you can do it for free: https://kdp.amazon.com/self-publishing/help?topicId=A17W8UM0MMSQX6

It is very important that you have a properly formatted book. It's not enough that Kindle accepts the book, because the readers will complain if anything is off. Make sure you have a properly formatted Table of Contents, that any graphics or images are formatted correctly, that new chapters start on a new page, etc.

If you're totally stuck, there are some service providers who offer the formatting service as well.

Book Cover

The book cover is another important element. In fact, some marketers consider the cover to be the most important aspect of Kindle book marketing. You won't make any sales if your cover isn't nice. It should be clear enough to read the title and get a feel for the book even when looking through the thumbnails on the Amazon Kindle browse pages.

Do a search for books in your genre on Kindle and see what those covers look like. You'll probably see some that strike you as really well done and others that are extremely poor. Note what works and doesn't work. Emulate, not copy, the style that works.

There are many people who will create your Kindle cover for you - Fiverr.com is a popular place to hire cover designers. Make absolutely sure that the service provider owns the rights to use the photo or graphic they use on the cover. Better yet, buy them yourself from a stock photo site and provide them to the service provider to design for you.

There is also Kindle cover software out there that can work really nicely. KD Renegade is a nice one.

People really do judge a book by its cover, so make sure yours is great. You'll upload it through your Kindle publishing page and use it in your marketing.

Website

Your website is going to be a big part of your marketing. It's going to be part of your brand, so I suggest you register a domain representative of your author name instead of just one book. That way, you'll have regular readers who will be interested in your next release.

Take a look at the websites of your favorite authors. Which elements do you like? What do you think they could do better?

Then, I suggest you set up a self-hosted WordPress blog. You can add actual blog posts that talk about your process of writing. This will keep your site fresh and keep readers interested.

Chronicle your journey - your ups and your downs. Many readers like to get to know authors this way.

Also, include a contact page so readers can write with praise or questions. Relationship building is a big part of your success as an author. You want people to get to know, like, and trust you.

Write an About Me page. Include some fun details about yourself and your passion for writing. It's fine if you're using a pen name - use elements of your life or your pen name's life to create this page.

Other pages include a book collection page, a terms of service page, and any others you think would work well on your site. Again, you can use other authors' sites for inspiration.

Your Opt In Form

I'll talk more about list building a bit further on, but I wanted to include it near the section about your website. Your list building efforts will be a big part of your book marketing now and in the future. If you don't currently have an autoresponder service, I suggest you sign up for either GetResponse or Aweber. Both have great help documents that can give you a running start.

Set up a list for your author site and create a web form. Install the proper plugin (either Aweber's or GetResponse's plugin) into your WordPress installation. Then, paste the code and information the plugin asks for. I recommend you use the sidebar widget so the opt in form appears on every page of your site.

People aren't going to sign up for nothing, though. I suggest you write a freebie ebook or give away several chapters of your book to get the opt in. You're giving them a gift in exchange for their email address.

Why do you want their email address? You can email them about new blog posts, new books, new lower prices, special offers, ebook bundles...whatever you would like. Emailing your list keeps you at the top of their mind and ensures you get more sales. Get the opt in form ready for everyone who visits your site and you'll gain access to that traffic time and time again, instead of just once.

Social Media

Social media is also a big part of your strategy. You don't have to spend hours maintaining your accounts each day, but you should become known in the genre you are targeting. You want to build relationships with readers and other authors. Social media will help foster these relationships and help drive traffic to your website.

I suggest you sign up for a Twitter account, using your author name. Include your website's address in your profile, along with a compelling personal photo (or the photo you're using for your pen name) and background graphic. Start to find and follow others in your niche and genre. Find lists people have created that are relevant to your genre. Many people will follow you back.

Retweet and respond to others' tweets - you want them to notice you. Tweet about what you're writing, what's going on in your life, quotes you like, and more. Really make it personal, interesting, and fun. Do this for around 10-15 minutes per day and you'll soon have built up a great following on Twitter.

You should also create a Facebook page for your author name and brand. You can post about what you're working on, what's going on in your day, and share interesting graphics and others' posts. You can post on relevant pages as your own page. Make sure your page name is interesting and descriptive. People won't tend to click through to your page if it's just your name (assuming you're not already well known). Put something like "Your Name - Juicy Paranormal Romance Author." You'll get many more people clicking through to learn more about you and hopefully liking your page.

Don't forget to link to your website from your social media accounts. Tweet and post about your free book download (in the hopes of getting people to visit your site and opt in to your list). Post from your site to your social media accounts as well - you want to link everything together to help people find you and get to know you.

The thing to keep in mind with social media is that it's about relationships. It's not about spamming your book or your link. You need to get to know people in your niche and your genre and help them get to know you. This can be fairly time consuming at first. Just go in with a plan, don't get distracted, and allow your presence in social media to build up over time.

Book Sites

There are a variety of different author, reader, and book sites you can join to help people get to know you and your books. These sites are perfectly targeted so you'll be able to find those who are interested in what you have to share. Some of these sites allow you to advertise your book (like when it's on sale or free) and others allow you to run book giveaways. This can be a great way to get additional reviews (it's very important to have these) and exposure.

For now, I'll just cover two of the most important ones. GoodReads and LibraryThing.

Here is where you can read all about the GoodReads author program: http://www.goodreads.com/author/program

They offer a variety of ways for you to get additional exposure. I recommend you take advantage of all of them.

LibraryThing has some similar features for authors that you can take advantage of. Here is more information about what they offer to authors:

http://www.librarything.com/about/authors

Again, I recommend you take advantage of all of what they have to offer. It can really help you break into the community and get you a lot of exposure for next to no cost.

The Importance of List Building

Earlier, I mentioned that you should put an opt in form on your website. That's so you can collect email addresses you can mail with special offers, new books, new blog posts, free books, and more.

List building should actually be the focus of all your marketing. You don't just want to get people to visit your website one time. That's lost traffic. You want them to visit time and time again and to buy all of your books. But, they have to get to know you first. The best way to make that happen is to build a list.

This is something traditional publishers still get wrong. They neglect list building specifically for authors. When they do it, they don't do it in an enticing way, particularly for new authors. You might sign up for a David Baldacci email list because you really enjoy his work...regardless of whether you're getting anything in return. You're a lot less likely to do the same for authors you don't know. That's the boat you're in when people hear about your work or see your opt in form. You have to give them a great reason to do so. You need to optimize your opt in form and emails.

Optimize Your Opt In Form

Your autoresponder company will do a good job of helping you create the look of your opt in form. I want to make sure you don't go over the top with the options and information you choose to collect from your site visitors, though. I've seen author's opt in forms where they ask for things like your phone number and home address. That is completely unnecessary. Really, all you need is the email address.

Make sure you include enticing text as the headline. The benefit of them opting in is that they will receive a free download (or whatever you have decided). Make that very clear so they opt in. Think about it from their perspective - what's going to get them to enter their email address?

Creating a Squeeze Page

A squeeze page is a page with minimal, enticing text and an opt in form. It has one purpose -to get people to opt in to your list. Ideally, it won't have any other links or anything distracting at all. You can send people to this page from social media sites and other sites you list your email address on.

You may not be familiar with copywriting, but it will serve you well to familiarize yourself to it. Your squeeze page should include a headline and some bullet points that spell out the benefits of opting into your list. If they are getting a fiction book, you might put a very small amount of story there and ask them to opt in to receive the rest. Do whatever you need to do to whet their appetite so you get the opt in.

Writing Autoresponder Emails

There are two different kinds of emails when it comes to email marketing. There are autoresponder emails that are designed to be sent according to when someone has opted in.

Someone can opt in on Monday and get message one while someone else opts in on Wednesday and gets message one.

I suggest you include a welcome email, complete with their freebie book or other download (whatever you promised them). Introduce yourself and let them get to know you a little bit.

You can schedule several of these emails to go out one day after the next. You can space them out further if you want. That's what's brilliant about having an autoresponder service - it works on autopilot for you.

Give them a lot of value throughout the messages. Try to leave cliff-hangers and enticing thoughts throughout to get them 'trained' to read the next one you send out. The goal is to get them to love what you send out through these autoresponder emails so they read your broadcast emails as well.

Writing Broadcast Emails

Broadcast emails are typically more 'of the moment' than autoresponder emails. These go out to everyone at the same time. You'll use the broadcast email function on your autoresponder service whenever you have a special offer, a thought you want to share with your list, a new blog post, or whatever you like. Don't hesitate to inform your subscribers about your new and upcoming releases - link them directly to the Amazon page to buy. That's the whole goal of having a list, and it will drive your sales up dramatically. Often, all people need is a reminder to buy and they'll rush right over to do it.

If you have people from your email list buying it will zoom you up in Amazon's charts - leading to more people buying and more people checking out your website and opting in to your list.

That's why I consider this a snowball strategy. It gets easier to make sales and reach bestseller status every time you release a book.

What to Put in the Book to Get People to Buy

This is one of the biggest things I see authors and publishers getting wrong. They include the book in the Kindle file...and only the book. You're missing out on huge sales opportunities if you do that.

Here are some things you should also include in the Kindle file:

- A list of all your books, along with short and compelling descriptions

- A teaser for your next release
- A special offer to buy a series of books in a special bundle offer
- A link to your squeeze page for your free download (get them excited about the freebie so they visit)

None of this has to be very long...but it should be included. When you finish a book from an author you like you're probably interested in reading their other works or visiting their website while they are fresh in your mind. Sure, you might type their name into Google to find them but it's a lot easier if the link is there. The same goes for those who read your books - make it very easy for them to buy more from you and opt in to your list.

Format your book with these things included in the file. Download the Kindle previewer (the download version is more accurate than the online version they give you during the upload process) to make sure the book looks great.

Release Your Book

You have all of the preparatory stuff out of the way, now it's time to publish and release your book. At this point, you should have gotten reviewers (via GoodReads and

LibraryThing, if you followed their suggestions). If you have not, contact those who've already reviewed books in your niche and send them a copy as a gift.

Inform your social media accounts, write a blog post, and email your list that that book is published and ready to buy. Remind those who've promised reviews that you'd love their honest opinion early on so new readers get a feel for its quality before they buy. Sometimes reviewers need a little nudge.

Many people have a special, low launch price to get those early sales. You can raise or lower your price depending on how well the book is doing and what you want to test. The goal is to get those early sales no matter what so you can get into lists on Amazon and get linked to from around the site.

Free Days

If you join the KDP Select program through Kindle, you'll be able to list your book for free on certain days. This was a strategy that worked exceedingly well in years past. These days, the free book downloads count for very little when Amazon calculates your book's rank. Still, it counts for something, can get you exposure, can act as a loss leader to your other books (because you'll be cross-promoting them, of course), and can help you get more reviews.

Test out running free days. Mail your list about them, pass the word on social media, and contact free book blogs to get more exposure. Note that many blogs have changed their business model since Amazon changed how commissions work for those who refer free books.

Gone are the days where free books were all you needed to do to market your book. Still, don't overlook them as part of a bigger plan.

Series Books

By now, you've probably read that I refer to this as a snowball method because of how it starts small and grows until you achieve great success with less effort on Kindle. Releasing books as part of a series is a big part of that. People love to read books as part of series - they like familiar characters and topics. This is true for fiction and nonfiction.

If you only have one book planned per pen name, reconsider. There is a reason people are practically addicted to buying books by their favorite author. You want to become that favorite author. You want people to get really excited about the book you're going to release next. If you haven't already planned to write a series, now is the time to make those plans.

Compilations

You can also compile the books you release in a series. Instead of paying for each book, they can get a deal if they buy the books all in one. It's a great upsell and can net you more money. It also takes next to no time to compile the books - it's a win-win.

How to Get Reviews

I covered this a little earlier on, but getting reviews is such an important part of the process that I really want to emphasize it. If you see a book with no reviews compared to a book with ten reviews, you're much more likely to purchase the latter. The element of social proof can really make or break your book sales.

The first rule is...never buy reviews.

Here are ways you can get reviews on your book's Amazon listing:

- Contact reviewers who've reviewed similar books to see if they'd like a complimentary copy in exchange for their honest review

- Ask friends and family members who are interested in the topic

- Contact authors of similar books

- Use LibraryThing and GoodReads for exposure and reviews

- Put a note in your book asking readers to leave their honest thoughts

As a side note, don't respond to the bad reviews you receive. Nothing good comes from that! When you get a bad review, search for your favorite book or author on Amazon. Sort by their '1 star' reviews.

See? Even the very best get scathing reviews.

Make changes if you need to, take constructive criticism the way it was intended, and leave the rest.

Making Deals With Other Authors

There are some pretty cool ways to get additional exposure by making deals with other authors. Let's say you have a book that is complementary to another book - a book you know is selling decently well. Offer to put a link to that author's book in the back of your book, if they'll do the same with yours. This should help you get into related book lists.

Some might even review your book on their blog...give them a review copy and let them go at it. Some authors are afraid to do this because they think they'll get a bad review. Others are afraid of rubbing elbows with the competition. Neither should be a concern for you. Sure, you might find things to fix or get a review that was harsher than you expected - that's just part of being an author.

Getting Your Readers to Pass the Word Along

Some books take off like crazy because of word of mouth. Readers talk a lot about books they enjoy and got a lot out of. Don't be afraid to mail your list that you'd love for them to share news of your book with friends and family. Sometimes, all you have to do is ask.

The Snowball Effect

I urge you to not get discouraged if things don't take off immediately. If no one knows about your book, no one can buy your book. Take steps now to get the word out there about your book and yourself as an author and it will go long way for you now and in the long run.

Many authors give it a try for a few days but let things go beyond that. Don't let that happen to you. Make a list of the steps you're going to take to market your book. I've laid things out for you in a relatively streamlined manner, but you should always make adjustments according to your audience, book, and style.

Where to Go From Here

You've worked hard so far to get this off the ground! Give yourself a pat on the back. Things don't end now, though. It's time to get more books out there. The more books you have, the more exposure you'll have. People will find one book and want to know about the other books you have. They'll get excited about your new releases. Having one book up there is great, but you just can't stop there. Build yourself an empire of books and a rabid fan base and you'll live the life of your dreams, as a successfully published author.

Printed by Libri Plureos GmbH in Hamburg, Germany